Well-behaved women
seldom make history.
—Laurel Thatcher Ulrich

★ WOMEN WHO ★
★ BROKE THE RULES ★

Coretta Scott King

KATHLEEN KRULL

interior illustrations by
Laura Freeman

BLOOMSBURY
NEW YORK   LONDON   NEW DELHI   SYDNEY

~❧~

To Ann Diener, bookseller extraordinaire
at The Yellow Book Road

~❧~

First published in the United States of America in December 2015
by Bloomsbury Children's Books
www.bloomsbury.com

Bloomsbury is a registered trademark of Bloomsbury Publishing Plc

For information about permission to reproduce selections from this book, write to
Permissions, Bloomsbury Children's Books, 1385 Broadway, New York, New York 10018
Bloomsbury books may be purchased for business or promotional use. For information on bulk purchases please contact
Macmillan Corporate and Premium Sales Department at specialmarkets@macmillan.com

Library of Congress Cataloging-in-Publication Data
Krull, Kathleen.
Women who broke the rules : Coretta Scott King / by Kathleen Krull ; illustrated by Laura Freeman.
pages   cm
ISBN 978-0-8027-3827-1 (paperback) • ISBN 978-0-8027-3826-4 (hardcover)
1. King, Coretta Scott, 1927–2006—Juvenile literature. 2. African American women—Biography—Juvenile literature.
3. African Americans—Biography—Juvenile literature. 4. Civil rights workers—United States—Biography—Juvenile
literature. 5. Civil rights movements—United States—History—20th century—Juvenile literature. 6. King, Martin Luther, Jr.,
1929–1968—Juvenile literature. I. Freeman-Hines, Laura, illustrator. II. Title. III. Title: Coretta Scott King.
E185.97.K47K89 2015   323.092—dc23   [B]   2014032450

Art created digitally using Photoshop and Painter
Typeset in Beaufort
Book design by Nicole Gastonguay

Printed in China by Leo Paper Products, Heshan, Guangdong
2 4 6 8 10 9 7 5 3 1 (paperback)
2 4 6 8 10 9 7 5 3 1 (hardcover)

All papers used by Bloomsbury Publishing, Inc., are natural, recyclable products
made from wood grown in well-managed forests. The manufacturing processes
conform to the environmental regulations of the country of origin.

TABLE OF CONTENTS

S ome women break the rules. Others break the Rules—the racist laws that once kept blacks and whites strictly apart, especially in the Southern states.

Before the Rules were changed, life was all uphill for an African American girl in the rural South. Singing was one of the things that gave Coretta Scott the guts to climb up and over the Rules.

"My sister always sang," said Edythe Scott. "All of us sang—my mother sang, we sang together in choirs, in church, in school."

Coretta was born April 27, 1927, near Marion, Alabama. This was a farming community where the leaders were her family members. Her name came from two relatives, a grandmother Cora and an aunt Etta.

Slavery had ended sixty years earlier. But Rules were in place, Rules enforced by violence. Blacks still had different drinking fountains and bathrooms, swimming pools and parks, jobs, and parts of town to live in. At the movies they had to sit in the balcony. On buses they had to sit in the back and give up their seats if whites wanted them. Blacks were often prevented from voting, so it was hard to change things legally.

WHITES ONLY

Coretta was a bit sheltered at first, living on the family farm. But at the local ice cream store, while all the white kids got served, she had to stand at the back door with the other black kids. Then she couldn't even get what she wanted—only the flavors that were left over.

On visits to town, white kids would try to force the black kids off the sidewalks, and this scared Coretta.

Hurt, confused, and sometimes angry—that was how the unequal treatment made Coretta feel. Until her teens

she was known as a fighter, sometimes throwing sticks and stones at her siblings and cousins. She had "an uncontrollable temper," said Edythe, who probably knew it all too well.

Coretta's parents told her constantly that she was just as good as anyone else. Her father worked several jobs—farming, cutting hair, hauling lumber. He also ran a grocery store and built their house right next to it. He even owned his own truck. Whites who were jealous of his success often threatened him. Coretta grew up worrying that something could happen to him at any time.

Her mother was the pianist for the church choir and often let tiny Coretta sing solos. Coretta loved the family's old-fashioned record player. When she cranked it by hand, she could play albums of spirituals, gospel, jazz, and blues. She would listen for hours and sing along. It soothed her and made her less afraid.

She began helping on the farm at age six, feeding the cows and chickens. By ten, to earn money for school supplies, she was doing the hard work of hoeing, chopping, and picking rows of cotton on a neighbor's farm. Her dad bragged about her. She would spend Saturdays racing to pick two hundred pounds of cotton so she'd have time to practice her music later.

White grade schools had books, bathrooms, and buses to take students home. At Coretta's one-room school there were few books, no indoor bathrooms, and no buses. She walked the three miles to school every day, and then back.

But she loved school. By the time she finished first grade the teacher promoted her to third. In sixth grade she made a splash by reciting aloud "Paul Revere's Ride," all 130 lines of Henry Wadsworth Longfellow's poem.

The nearest black high school was ten miles away. At first she stayed with a family in town. Then her mom—the first black woman to drive a car in the area—became a school bus driver and took her back and forth.

Coretta blossomed in the school's strong music program. Her teachers taught her about classical music and all the leading black performers of the day. They sent students out of state to give concerts, performing works like George Frideric Handel's *Messiah*.

She couldn't get enough. She learned to play the piano, trumpet, violin, and several other instruments. By fifteen she was the pianist and choir director for her church. It was obvious that her genius was for singing. Her voice was like a clear and powerful liquid.

To Coretta, music wasn't just a matter of notes on a page. It went deeper. She saw how music soothed both black and white audiences, how it stirred emotion.

As a friend observed, "She was on a higher plane than most of the people her age."

Music put her there.

WOWING THE CROWD 2

After graduating at the top of her class, she decided she *must* get more education in music, maybe even become a concert singer.

But how? In her day, 1945, hardly any women of any race went on to college.

Coretta's parents were the ones who made it happen.

Her mother had been forced to leave school when she was in fourth grade. She told Coretta that nothing was more important than college. "You get an education and try to be somebody," she said. "Then you won't have to be kicked around by anybody, and you won't have to depend on anyone for your livelihood, not even a man."

Her father, the grandson of a slave, had left school in sixth grade. He felt exactly the same. He told his daughters they could do anything a man could do.

Coretta's strong older sister inspired her. Edythe was then the only black to attend Antioch College in Yellow Springs, Ohio. She won a scholarship and traveled to the North, where the Rules were not so harsh. Coretta followed her, also on scholarship, one of three blacks in her class of a hundred or so.

The college's motto was rather stern: "Be ashamed to die until you have won some victory for humanity." But Coretta found that it helped build her confidence. She needed extra tutoring at first but was soon making straight As.

Everyone expected her to date the one black man in her class. Instead she dated a white student who loved music as much as she did.

In between appearing in Gilbert and Sullivan operettas and other events, she studied. She trained in both music and education. That way she could support herself as a teacher in case a career in singing didn't work out.

Two years of practice teaching were required. Her first year went fine, as she taught in the private school run by the college. Naturally, she did a lot of singing and making up tunes with her students.

Her second year was thorny. The local public school turned her down because she would have been the only black teacher. Coretta was furious at this unexpected Rule. She fought back, complaining to her college president.

But he refused to help. And Coretta refused to teach at the all-black school she was sent to. To get her degree, she taught at the college school again.

After this, she got active in the National Association for

the Advancement of Colored People (NAACP) and other groups that were working to change the Rules.

Her dream was to follow in the footsteps of Marian Anderson, a powerful singer who'd made Rule-breaking history. Paul Robeson, then the world's most famous black singer, was also a role model for her. He used his unusually deep voice to speak out for social justice—against the Rules.

When Coretta gave her first solo public concert in 1948, her sublime singing wowed the crowd. At another concert, she was put on the same program with none other than Paul Robeson. He couldn't have been more impressed. He saw a future star in her and urged her to get all the training she possibly could.

Three years later, Coretta was on her way. The New England Conservatory of Music in Boston had accepted her. Her proud father was happy to pay her tuition, but at age twenty-four, she wanted to do this on her own. After applying for scholarships like mad, she boarded her train to Boston.

She was confident about her future—though still without a clue about how she was going to pay for it.

While waiting to switch trains in New York, Coretta called home to say hi. A letter had just arrived. She had won a grant that would pay for her school tuition, though not her living expenses.

She found ways to make her new life work. She bargained with her landlady, cleaning the house in exchange for break-fast and rent. She scrimped and took various part-time jobs. Sometimes dinner was a matter of peanut butter with gra-ham crackers.

Her time was stretched thin, but she was just plain jazzed to be fulfilling her dreams. Classmates marveled at her poise. "Singing put her up there, in front of an audience, preparing her to be an actor with her voice," said one. "She had a wonderful presence."

In 1952, about six months into her degree, a friend fixed her up with a guy she thought Coretta might like.

Martin Luther King Jr. was a young black minister and a religious studies student at Boston University. Coretta wasn't hopeful—the ministers she knew back home weren't exactly fun. But she said okay.

They went to lunch at a café that served home-cooked Southern food. On her part, it wasn't love at first sight. Martin was shorter than she liked, and also two years younger than she was.

And he was kind of bold. While driving her back to school, he blurted that she had all he wanted in a wife: character, intelligence, personality, and beauty. Mention of marriage on a first date gave Coretta the jitters.

But their talk over lunch had certainly been intense. He had the bravest of plans for the future—fighting to overcome the Rules, the unfair treatment of blacks. This fight was not going to use violence. The best way to change minds was just the opposite: nonviolence—peaceful, forceful resistance. Martin made it all sound possible.

Coretta didn't quite

realize it at the time, but this man was one of the most per-
suasive speakers on the planet. He had learned from his
father, a famous preacher. And now he was using his way
with words on her.

They kept dating. On one date she listened to him preach
at a nearby church and was electrified at his skill. On another
date he took her to a symphony concert, knowing she'd
love it.

They also went dancing—and he was an excellent dancer.

It took her six months to accept his proposal. She was torn. Some of her friends weren't sure he was worthy of her. Being a minister's wife didn't appeal to her. Nor did moving back to the South, where Martin felt he could make the biggest difference. Mainly, she wanted to get a degree in music and start a career using her voice. She did want a husband and children—someday.

In her time, women rarely got to have both a career and a family. Plus pursuing Martin's goals with him represented "Adventure" with a capital *A*, and "Change" with a capital *C*.

So the answer was yes. She wanted to be an equal partner in their marriage, while he was more traditional, preferring a stay-at-home wife. They hadn't quite worked that part out before the wedding.

They were married in 1953 in Alabama. Martin's father performed the ceremony, agreeing to remove the word "obey" from Coretta's vows. It was a most unusual request at the time.

No local hotels would accept African Americans. They spent their wedding night at a friend's house. Their friend was an undertaker, so technically the honeymoon was in a funeral home.

Coretta couldn't wait to get back to her classes. She earned a degree in voice and violin, while Martin finished up his degree and shared the household chores.

Then the Kings moved to Montgomery, Alabama, where Martin had accepted a job. One of their first purchases? A piano.

While Martin established his ministry, Coretta organized all the church's musical activities. She also began performing in public. She wasn't on the national stages she had dreamed of, but in local churches and small theaters. She sang spirituals and introduced classical music to audiences that loved her, and kept giving concerts when possible.

Being a minister's wife turned out to be a full-time job. She was good at it, able to help and talk with all kinds of people, always representing Martin, and giving him feedback on his sermons.

Their home was not especially private. They basically shared it with the church community, and various groups used it as a meeting place. The phone rang constantly, with people needing help, or offering help, or yelling a string of bad words. Martin was already making enemies among whites.

In 1955, Coretta had the first of their four children. Only two weeks later, they got an urgent call.

It was about a woman who'd been to Coretta's concerts and didn't yet realize she was married to a rising young minister.

The woman's name was Rosa Parks.

Rosa Parks was the brave woman arrested for refusing to give up her seat on the bus to a white person. Since most bus passengers were black, this Rule was particularly racist.

Black leaders agreed that now was the time to unify and send a message: they should boycott—or stop riding—the city's buses until Montgomery changed its Rule. Martin approved of this nonviolent way of protest, and his church became the boycott's headquarters.

Martin and Coretta were the key organizers. When she couldn't attend meetings because of the baby, he filled her in. She handled all the phone calls, helping those who needed rides. To stay off the buses, people carpooled, took taxis, walked, rode mules, or hitched horses to a buggy.

On the first morning of the boycott, she got up extra early to watch the first buses pass by. Hooray—they were empty! The boycott was working. The city could not afford to send empty buses around and would have to change its policy.

Still, Coretta couldn't help worrying about Martin. In his speeches about the boycott, he was becoming a target for

white rage. But she remained calm no matter how scared she was inside.

Martin once called their marriage a "cosmic companionship"—they each knew they were serving a cause much larger than themselves. Coretta later recalled thinking: "What a blessing, to be a coworker with a man whose life would have so profound an impact on the world."

While he was at meetings, she insisted she was fine alone at night with the baby. But church members took turns visiting her, and one of them was there the night a bomb was hurled onto the Kings' porch. Coretta and the baby weren't

hurt, but an angry crowd gathered outside their house, planning revenge on the bombers.

Martin rushed home and gave a soothing speech. He brought Coretta outside and showed the crowd how calm she was. Everyone else should follow her example—violence was not the answer.

Both Martin's and Coretta's parents begged them to leave the city after this, but Coretta refused.

Eventually, Montgomery officials were desperate to stop the boycott. They went to court, and the case went all the way to the Supreme Court. In 1956, its decision came:

Alabama's separation of blacks and whites on its buses was unconstitutional. It violated the legal rights of African Americans.

The boycott was an eye-opening success. It is considered the birth of the civil rights movement to gain blacks their rights under the law.

For the Kings, though, it meant more hateful calls, with Coretta working harder to stay calm.

She leaned on music for support. On the first anniversary of the boycott, she took a leading role in a large concert, performing with stars like Duke Ellington and Harry Belafonte. She sang classical pieces, then told the story of the boycott in story and song. She was nervous at first, but the audience was—as always—wowed.

She had found a splendid way to combine her two loves—music and civil rights.

While Coretta raised their four children, Martin was off speaking as many as two hundred days a year. He sent her flowers and mushy valentines when he was away.

Several times he was arrested at demonstrations or on false charges. Worried for his safety in jail, Coretta wouldn't waste a minute. She would go straight to the top for help, calling officials in a position to rescue him.

"My wife was always stronger than I was through the struggle," Martin wrote. "In the darkest moments, she always brought the light of hope."

Sometimes they clashed because Martin, as well as the men he worked with, believed a woman's place was in the home. Some of the men called Coretta "Queen" when they thought she meddled too much. But when she could line up a friend or relative as a babysitter, she went with Martin on trips. Sometimes she took his place at speeches if he was away on more urgent business.

As often as possible, especially at Christmas, Coretta was able to gather the whole family around the piano to sing. But mostly she was on her own, supervising the kids' games of Scrabble, watching over all her children's friends who hung out at their house, and keeping everyone behaved in public when all they wanted to do was wiggle out of their chairs.

Coretta tried to protect them from the Rules. But it was hard explaining why they couldn't go to white playgrounds. Or, when they were giddy about an amusement park called Funtown, which didn't allow blacks, why they couldn't go. When Funtown did admit blacks in 1963, Martin and Coretta finally took their kids and had a grand time going on all the rides.

That same year, Coretta took part in the momentous March on Washington. This was a peaceful gathering at the capital to protest the Rules in the most visible way possible.

About a quarter of a million Americans, about three out of ten of them white, streamed in from all over the country to take part.

Coretta was hurt that the wives of the leaders were not allowed to march along with their husbands—usually at marches she walked hand in hand with Martin. And it bothered her that no woman was allowed to speak from the stage, not even Rosa Parks.

But Coretta did sit on the platform behind Martin as he ended the day with one of the most famous speeches in history. She witnessed him calling on people to go home and

keep working toward his dream that someday all Americans would be free.

Martin's words touched many who hadn't given civil rights much thought yet. Less than a year later, the Rules *finally* began breaking down.

President Lyndon Johnson signed the Civil Rights Act of 1964. It called for the government to make sure that blacks could attend public schools, be served in public places, and have the chance to obtain decent jobs.

Then came the Voting Rights Act of 1965, promising government enforcement of blacks' right to vote.

By now Coretta and Martin had really lost their privacy. They learned that everything they said could be overheard, making it hard to speak normally. The Federal Bureau of Investigation (FBI), a government agency, decided that Martin was a potential enemy of America. In an invasion of privacy unusual at the time, the FBI listened to the Kings' phone calls and bugged their home with tiny microphones.

They followed every move of Martin's—and Coretta's, too. By now she was known as the first lady of the civil rights

movement. But she already had a second cause—world peace. She opposed America's involvement in the Vietnam War before Martin did. Her antiwar stance put her on the FBI's radar.

Coretta looked for more ways to contribute. She decided to give a series of concerts to raise money. Martin's organization badly needed money for staff, travel, and bail if anyone was arrested.

Some on his staff pooh-poohed her idea at first. They changed their minds when she began turning over her earnings.

For the next several years, she performed in thirty concerts in all the finest halls. She called them Freedom Concerts.

Wearing an elegant dress, Coretta wove story, poetry, and song into the saga of the civil rights movement. The concerts were divided into sections like "The Dream Blighted," "Supreme Sacrifices," and "The March on Washington." She always ended by singing "We Shall Overcome," the spiritual that became the movement's theme song.

The evenings were magical. Thousands would show up, jumping to their feet to give her standing ovations. Besides money, Coretta raised awareness—especially in areas that were new to the struggle, like the West Coast.

She was winning people's hearts with music. Not marches or politics or demonstrations—but music.

WOMEN POWER

Then came the day Coretta Scott King had dreaded most. In 1968 her husband was shot and killed.

People feared for this brokenhearted widow with four young children. But as her sister said, Coretta had "a core of inner strength few people have possessed."

Coretta spent the first six days after Martin's assassination comforting others. She also cautioned against the rage that many blacks felt. "You can't fight if you have anger," she warned.

Then, even before her husband was buried, she took his place as the leader of a march. With her three oldest children, she walked in support of black garbage workers in Memphis. People all over the world marveled at her courage.

One week after Martin's death, President Johnson signed the Civil Rights Act of 1968. This made it illegal to refuse to sell a house in a white neighborhood to a black person. It was another milestone in the cause of equality.

Now forty years old, Coretta marched on.

She fulfilled Martin's speaking invitations, calling on everyone to carry on his work. At first she used his words, then her own. Those who hadn't heard her speak before couldn't believe how inspiring she was.

Within months she founded the Martin Luther King Jr. Center for Nonviolent Social Change, known as the King Center. She raised some of the money for it with more Freedom Concerts.

Over the years, she seemed to be everywhere at once. She traveled the world, meeting with leaders, giving speeches as a champion for those without a voice. Sometimes she worked eighteen-hour days.

In some ways Coretta broadened her husband's scope. She became a human rights activist who took stands on many issues.

She called upon American women "to unite and form a solid block of women power to fight the three great evils of racism, poverty, and war." She never changed her stance on nonviolence and was opposed to any war. She came out against the death penalty, and for gun control, gay marriage, and universal health care.

In 1983, after years of Coretta's campaigning, Dr. Martin Luther King Jr.'s birthday was made a national holiday. President Ronald Reagan signed the bill with multiple pens, which were then passed out to Coretta and the other witnesses as mementos. A day for everyone to celebrate freedom, it has become used as a day of service, of doing volunteer work in Martin's name.

Coretta received honorary degrees from more than sixty colleges and universities. She might have been proudest of her award from Antioch College, which called her "one of the most influential women leaders in the world."

She was not wealthy, and celebrities sometimes helped her out. Talk-show host Oprah Winfrey bought Coretta a condo in the same Atlanta building as singers Janet Jackson and Elton John.

She never really retired, with plans for the future that included recording an album.

After a stroke and while battling cancer, Coretta went to a hospital for alternative medicine in Rosarito Beach, Mexico. She died there on January 30, 2006, at age seventy-eight.

Four of the five living presidents attended her funeral, plus notables of every kind, including future president Barack Obama. President George W. Bush spoke: "By going forward with a strong and forgiving heart, Coretta Scott King not only secured her husband's legacy, she built her own. Having loved a leader, she became a leader."

Her name lives on in many ways—including children's books. The American Library Association established the Coretta Scott King Award for books that uphold her values. As important as the Newbery and Caldecott Awards, it honors African American writers and illustrators. The list of winners includes some of the most beautiful and distinguished books for children.

In trying to make a better world, Coretta gave a voice to the voiceless, including young people. "I think what I've tried to do is to empower people to understand that they can make a difference," she said. She called on future generations "to use your success to help create this beautiful symphony of brotherhood and sisterhood."

Music, in other words, could keep everyone marching.

★ SOURCES AND FURTHER READING ★

Books
(* especially for young readers)

Bagley, Edythe Scott. *Desert Rose: The Life and Legacy of Coretta Scott King*. Tuscaloosa: University of Alabama Press, 2012.

* Bankston, John. *Coretta Scott King and the Story Behind the Coretta Scott King Award*. Newark, DE: Mitchell Lane, 2003.

Collier-Thomas, Bettye, and V.P. Franklin. *Sisters in the Struggle: African-American Women in the Civil Rights–Black Power Movement*. New York: New York University Press, 2001.

Crawford, Vicki, Jacqueline Rouse, and Barbara Woods. *Women in the Civil Rights Movement: Trailblazers and Torchbearers, 1941–1965*. New York: Carlson Publishing, 1990.

King, Coretta Scott. *My Life with Martin Luther King, Jr*. New York: Henry Holt, 1993.

King, Dexter Scott. *Growing Up King: An Intimate Memoir*. New York: Intellectual Properties Management, 2003.

* McCarty, Laura T. *Coretta Scott King: A Biography*. Westport, CT: Greenwood Press, 2009.

* McPherson, Stephanie Sammartino. *Coretta Scott King*. Minneapolis: Twenty-First Century Books, 2008.

* Sharp, Anne Wallace. *Coretta Scott King*. Detroit: Lucent, 2009.

Websites

About Mrs. King, The King Center: **thekingcenter.org/about-mrs-king**

Antioch College: **antiochcollege.org**

Civil Rights Movement Vets: **www.crmvet.org**

Coretta Scott King Book Awards: **www.ala.org/emiert/cskbookawards**

Coretta Scott King Interview with the Academy of Achievement:
www.achievement.org/autodoc/page/kin1int-1

Martin Luther King Jr. Day of Service: **mlkday.gov**

Martin Luther King Jr. Research and Education Institute: **mlk-kpp01.stanford.edu**

National Association for the Advancement of Colored People: **www.naacp.org**